D0326029

THE WISDOM OF
ANCIENT
ROME

Compiled by Benoît Desombres

Abbeville Press   Publishers

New York   London   Paris

Cover illustration and vignettes by Danielle Siegelbaum

For the English-language edition
RESEARCH, TRANSLATION FROM THE FRENCH, AND BIBLIOGRAPHY:
John O'Toole
EDITOR: Jacqueline Decter
TYPOGRAPHIC DESIGN: Virginia Pope
PRODUCTION EDITOR: Owen Dugan

For the original edition
SERIES EDITORS: Marc de Smedt and Michel Piquemal
DESIGNER: Dominique Guillaumin/Cédric Ramadier

First edition
10 9 8 7 6 5 4 3 2 1

Library of Congress Cataloging-in-Publication Data

Paroles de la Rome antique. English.
The wisdom of ancient Rome/compiled by Benoît Desombres.
p. cm.
Includes bibliographical references.
ISBN 0-7892-0242-5
1. Quotations, Latin—Translations into English. I. Desombres,
Benoît. II. Title.
PN6080.P1713 1996
089'.71—dc20   96–17065

The Romans proved to be great soldiers, great builders, great jurists, great poets. But were they great thinkers? Did they formulate original thought?

At first glance, the answer seems to be in doubt, because the wisdom of ancient Rome is pervaded by the major currents of Greek thought. Thus Lucretius takes Epicurus as his authority, while Seneca shows himself faithful to the Stoics. It was the Greeks who came up with the theme on which the Romans in turn composed their own variations, and that theme is: follow Nature and we will be content. He who knows Nature finds therein the rule for a good life and the secret of simple happiness.

Despite the nuances and divergences distinguishing the various schools of thought in ancient Rome, a common inspiration runs throughout their philosophical texts. They are fired by the idea of Nature, which represents the entire universe in a state of perfection. Nature is one: it unites Heaven and Earth, connecting human beings with the stars and bringing them all together in a single family. Nature is beautiful: details, which occasionally shock at first, delight us when we understand how they contribute to the overall harmony of the whole. Finally, Nature is ordered; a divine law determines its arrangement, namely, the subordination of the means to the ends, and the parts to the whole.

Within Nature, human nature occupies a specific place that it has been assigned. It is a place the wise man knows how to keep by avoiding the follies of those who, through pride or cowardice, would either surpass man or belittle him.

Yet we must also recognize what the Romans themselves contributed that was wholly their own. They translated, and therefore transposed into the genius of their tongue, the intuitions of the Greeks. Thanks to these Romans, Latin became the language of philosophers for centuries thereafter. By developing the idea of *humanitas*, they expressed a humanism with a universal aim. This idea encompasses both the dignity of every human being, and a benevolent openness to all. The term also means "virtue," the specific excellence of those who remain faithful to their nature, within whom the soul controls the body and the mind, anger and desire.

Some readers might be surprised to find Marcus Aurelius and Epictetus among the authors quoted here. Although both wrote in Greek, not Latin, they rightly belong to the Roman world and represent above all the two extremes of the social hierarchy under the Empire: Epictetus had been a slave in Rome before being emancipated, while Marcus Aurelius ruled as emperor. A man's greatness and the power of his thought and wisdom are indeed independent of his social condition.

In our century, when humans are relentlessly working to master and exploit the earth, it is good to listen to those who speak to us of a peaceful and respectful relationship with Nature. In our century, when men have torn and continue to tear themselves to pieces, it is good to meditate on the solidarity of the human race.

 Benoît Desombres

We Possess Nothing

Never say about anything, "I have lost it," but only "I have given it back." Is your child dead? It has been given back. Is your wife dead? She has been given back. "I have had my farm taken away." Very well, this too has been given back. "Yet it was a rascal who took it away." But what concern is it of yours by whose instrumentality the Giver called for its return? So long as He gives it you, take care of it as of a thing that is not your own, as travelers treat their inn.

Epictetus, *The Manual*

Love Punished, fresco

True Charity

All else which I would have those who feel pity do, he will do gladly and with a lofty spirit; he will bring relief to another's tears, but will not add his own; to the shipwrecked man he will give a hand, to the exile shelter, to the needy alms; he will not do as most of those who wish to be thought pitiful do—fling insultingly their alms, and scorn those whom they help, and shrink from contact with them—but he will give as a man to his fellow man out of the common store.

Seneca, *On Mercy*

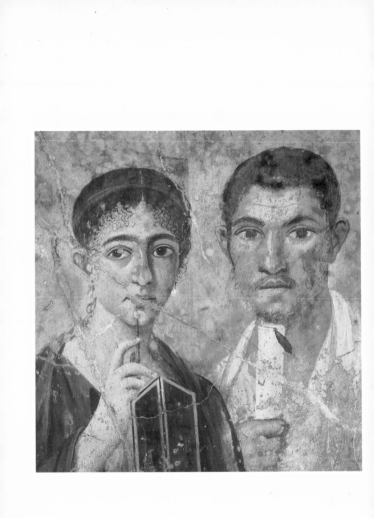

Nothing will ever please me, no matter how excellent or beneficial, if I must retain the knowledge of it to myself.

No good thing is pleasant to possess without friends to share it.

No one can live happily who looks to himself alone and transforms everything into a question of his own utility; you must live for you neighbor, if you wish to live for yourself.

Seneca, *Letters to Lucilius*

Paquius Proculus, a Wealthy Baker, and His Wife, fresco

The Proper Measure

Each man's body is a measure for his property, just as the foot is a measure for his shoe. If, then, you abide by this principle, you will maintain the proper measure, but if you go beyond it, you cannot help but fall headlong over a precipice, as it were, in the end. So

Perseus Freeing Andromeda, fresco

also in the case of your shoe; if once you go beyond
the foot, you get first a gilded shoe, then a purple one,
then an embroidered one. For once you go beyond the
measure there is no limit.

Epictetus, *The Manual*

On the Advantage of Being Ill

We are never so virtuous as when we are ill. Has a sick man ever been tempted by greed or lust? He is neither a slave to his passions nor ambitious for office; he cares nothing for wealth and is content with the little he has, knowing that he must leave it. It is then that he remembers the gods and realizes that he is mortal: he feels neither envy, admiration, nor contempt for any man: not even slanderous talk can win his attention or give him food for thought, and his dreams are all of baths and cool springs. These are his sole concern, the object of all his prayers; meanwhile he resolves that if he is lucky enough to recover he will lead a gentle and easy life in the future, that is, a life of happy innocence. So here for our guidance is the rule, put shortly, which the philosophers seek to express in endless words and volumes: in health we should continue to be the men we vowed to become when sickness prompted our words.

Pliny the Younger, *Letters*

Fantastic Architecture, fresco

Why are you angry with your slave, you with your master?...Wait a little. Behold, death comes, who will make you equals....

The end, all too soon, threatens the victor and the vanquished. Rather let us spend the little time that is left in respose and peace! Let no man loathe us when we lie a corpse....

Can you wish for the victim of your wrath a greater ill than death? Even though you do not move a finger, he will die. You waste your pains if you wish to do what needs must be....

Soon shall we spew forth this frail spirit. Meanwhile, so long as we draw breath, so long as we live among men, let us cherish humanity. Let us not cause fear to any man, nor danger; let us scorn losses, wrongs, abuse, and taunts, and let us endure with heroic mind our short-lived ills. While we are looking back, as they say, and turning around, straightway death will be upon us.

Seneca, *On Anger*

Brawl between Pompeians and Nucerians at the Amphitheater of Pompeii

Lead a Good Life

M en do not care how nobly they live, but only how long, although it is within the reach of every man to live nobly, but within no man's power to live long....

Many have gone through life merely accumulating the instruments of life. Consider individuals, survey men in general: there is none whose life does not look forward to the morrow. "What harm is there in this," you ask. Infinite harm; for such persons do not live, but are preparing to live. They postpone everything.

Seneca, *Letters to Lucilius*

Bust of a Young Man, marble marquetry

What Troubles Humans

It is not the things themselves that disturb men, but their judgments about these things. For example, death is nothing dreadful...but the judgment that death is dreadful, *this* is the dreadful thing. When, therefore, we are hindered, or disturbed, or grieved, let us never blame anyone but ourselves, that means, our own judgments. It is the part of an uneducated person to blame others where he himself fares ill; to blame himself is the part of one whose education has begun; to blame neither another nor his own self is the part of one whose education is already complete.

Epictetus, *The Manual*

Equality of Human Beings

I am a man: nothing human is alien to me.

Terence, *The Self-Tormentor*

All humans, the best and the others, deserve respect.

Cicero, *On Moral Obligation*

If there is any good in philosophy, it is this: that it never looks into pedigrees. All men, if traced back to their original source, spring from the gods. . . .The senate chamber is not open to all; the army, too, is scrupulous in choosing those whom it admits to toil and danger. But a noble mind is free to all men.

Seneca, *Letters to Lucilius*

The Carpenter, fresco

The Human Family

What is our purpose? What precepts do we offer? Should we bid them refrain from bloodshed? What a little thing it is not to harm one whom you ought to help! It is indeed worthy of great praise, when man treats man with kindness! Shall we advise holding out our hand to the shipwrecked, or pointing out the way to the wanderer, or sharing a crust with the starving?...

I can lay down for mankind a rule in concise form for our duties in human relationships: all that you behold, that which comprises both god and man, is one—we are the parts of one great body. Nature made us members of one family, since she created us from the same source and to the same end. She engendered in us mutual affection, and made us prone to friendships. She established fairness and justice; according to her ruling, it is more wretched to commit than to suffer injury. Through her orders, let our hands be ready for all that needs to be helped.

Seneca, *Letters to Lucilius*

Primavera, fresco

Serve Humanity

From this impulse is developed the sense of mutual attraction which unites human beings as such; this also is bestowed by nature. The mere fact of their common humanity requires that one man should feel another man to be akin to him.... We are by nature fitted to form unions, societies, and states.

The Stoics hold that the universe is governed by divine will; it is a city or state of which both men and gods are members, and each one of us is a part of this universe; from which it is a natural consequence that we should prefer the common advantage to our own....The traitor to his country does not deserve greater reprobation than the man who betrays the common advantage or security for the sake of his own advantage or security.

Cicero, *On the Ends of Goods and Evils*

Illusionistic Wall Decoration in the Villa of the Mysteries

The Specific Quality of Man

No man ought to glory except in that which is his own. We praise a vine if it makes the shoots teem with increase, if by its weight it bends to the ground the very poles which hold its fruit; would any man prefer to this vine one from which golden grapes and golden leaves hang down?

In a vine the virtue peculiarly its own is fertility; in man also we should praise that which is his own. Suppose that he has a retinue of comely slaves and a beautiful house, that his farm is large and large his income; none of these things is in the man himself, they are all on the outside. Praise the quality in him which cannot be given or snatched away, that which is the peculiar property of the man.

Do you ask what this is? It is soul, and reason brought to perfection in the soul. For man is a reasoning animal. Therefore, man's highest good is attained if he has fulfilled the good for which nature designed him at birth.

And what is it which this reason demands of him? The easiest thing in the world: to live in accordance with his own nature.

Seneca, *Letters to Lucilius*

Portrait of a Woman with Stylus

Invincible Freedom

For though the laws be overborne by some one individual's power, though the spirit of freedom be intimidated, still sooner or later they assert themselves either through unvoiced public sentiment, or through secret ballots disposing of some high office of state. Freedom suppressed and again regained bites with keener fangs than freedom never endangered.

Cicero, *On Moral Obligation*

Cupid, fresco in the Villa of the Mysteries

God is near you, he is with you, he is within you.... A holy spirit indwells within us, one who marks our good and bad deeds, and is our guardian. As we treat this spirit, so are we treated by it. Indeed, no man can be good without the help of God. Can one rise superior to fortune unless God helps him to rise? He it is that gives noble and upright counsel. In each good man "a god doth dwell, but what god know we not."[1]

If ever you have come upon a grove that is full of ancient trees which have grown to an unusual height, shutting out a view of the sky by a veil of pleached and intertwining branches, then the loftiness of the forest, the seclusion of the spot, and your marvel at the thick unbroken shade in the midst of the open spaces, will prove to you the presence of deity.... We worship the sources of mighty rivers; we erect altars at places where great streams burst suddenly from hidden sources; we adore springs of hot water as divine, and consecrate certain pools because of their dark waters or their immeasurable depth....

When a soul rises superior to other souls...when it passes through every experience as if it were of small account, when it smiles at our fears and at our prayers, it is stirred by a force from heaven. A thing like this cannot stand upright unless it be propped by the divine.

Seneca, *Letters to Lucilius*

[1]Virgil, *The Aeneid*   *Tavern Sign*

Natural Law and Divine Law

There is in fact a true law—namely, right reason—which is in accordance with nature, applies to all men, and is unchangeable and eternal. By its commands this law summons men to the performance of their duties; by its prohibitions it restrains them from doing wrong. Its commands and prohibitions always influence good men, but are without effect upon the bad. To invalidate this law by human legislation is never morally right, nor is it permissible ever to restrict its operation, and to annul it wholly is impossible. Neither the senate nor the people can absolve us from our obligation to obey this law....It will not lay down one rule at Rome and another at Athens, nor will it be one rule today and another tomorrow.

But there will be one law, eternal and unchangeable, binding at all times upon all peoples; and there will be, as it were, one common master and ruler of men, namely God, who is the author of this law, its interpreter, and its sponsor. The man who will not obey it will abandon his better self, and, in denying the true nature of a man, will thereby suffer the severest of penalties, though he has escaped all the other consequences which men call punishment.

Cicero, *On the Commonwealth*

Scenes on the Nile, mosaic

Love Nature

Everything is fitting for me, O Universe, which fits your purpose. Nothing in your good time is too early or too late for me.

Everything is fruit for me which your seasons, Nature, bear; from you, in you, to you are all things.

Earth loves the rain. The glorious ether loves to fall in rain. The Universe, too, loves to create what is to be. Therefore I say to the Universe, "Your love is mine."

Marcus Aurelius, *Meditations*

Detail of a Still Life

All of Nature Is Beautiful

Ears of corn, too, when they bend downwards, the lion's wrinkled brow, the foam flowing from the boar's mouth, and many other characteristics that are far from beautiful if we look at them in isolation, do nevertheless, because they follow from Nature's processes, lend those a further ornament and a fascination. And so, if a man has a feeling for, and a deeper insight

Battle of the Pygmies and Wild Beasts

into, the processes of the Universe, there is hardly one but will somehow appear to present itself pleasantly to him, even among mere attendant circumstances. Such a man also will feel no less pleasure in looking at the actual jaws of wild beasts than at the imitations which painters and sculptors exhibit, and he will be enabled to see in an old woman or an old man a kind of freshness and bloom.

Marcus Aurelius, *Meditations*

The Art of Nature

Nature has no external space; now the wonderous part of her art is that though she has circumscribed herself, everything within her which appears to decay and grow old and be useless she changes into herself, and again makes new things from these very same, so that she requires neither substance from without, nor wants a place into which she may cast that which decays. She is content then with her own space, and her own matter and her own art.

Marcus Aurelius, *Meditations*

Like a Ripe Olive

See always how ephemeral and cheap are the things of man—yesterday, a spot of albumen, tomorrow, ashes or a mummy. Therefore make your passage through this span of time in obedience to Nature and gladly lay down your life, as an olive, when ripe, might fall, blessing her who bore it and grateful to the tree which gave it life.

Marcus Aurelius, *Meditations*

A Priestess, detail

Like an Actor in a Play

Remember that you are an actor in a play, the character of which is determined by the Playwright: if He wishes the play to be short, it is short; if long, it is long; if He wishes you to play the part of a beggar, remember to act even this role adroitly; and so if your role be that of a cripple, an official, or a layman. For this is your business, to play admirably the role assigned you; but the selection of that role is Another's.

Epictetus, *The Manual*

Like a Cliff

Be like the cliff against which the waves continually break;

Naval Battle

...ut it stands firm and tames the fury of the water around it.

Marcus Aurelius, *Meditations*

The Frescos of Pompeii

The eruption of Vesuvius in A.D. 79 completely buried Pompeii, paradoxically immortalizing this flourishing city of twenty thousand inhabitants. Through the work of archaeologists, the entire hidden life of a fashionable ancient Roman city situated in the present-day region of Campania was eventually brought to light, frozen in time for eternity.

Pompeii represents a happy union of architecture and decoration. Visitors cannot help but marvel at the city's innumerable frescoes, which offer a mirror image of the Romans' day-to-day civil and religious life.

Yet beyond their being a striking record of a vanished civilization, the frescoes of Pompeii clearly form the most beautiful artistic expression of the distinctive spirit characterizing the Latin world.

Photography credits

© Lauros-Giraudon: pages 6, 32, 36, 38–39, 40.

© Alinari-Giraudon: pages 10, 14, 26, 28.

© Photo Bulloz: pages 8, 12–13, 16, 20, 24, 44.

© Edimédia: pages 18, 22, 30, 42 (photo Loren), 46–47.

Selected Bibliography

All the literature, philosophy, and history of ancient Greece and Rome is published in the scholarly and solid Loeb Classical Library, a series of bilingual editions offering a good English translation that rarely strays from the original text printed on the facing page.

At times overly formal, the English of the Loeb translations may not be to everyone's liking. Penguin Classics offers affordable paperback editions of a good number of the Latin writers in reliable English translations. We might also mention the Greek and Latin Classics series published by Cambridge University Press, along with their Texts in the History of Political Thought series.

See in particular:

Cicero, *De re publica: Selections.* James Zetzel, ed. Cambridge Greek and Latin Classics Series. Cambridge, England: Cambridge University Press, 1995.

Cicero, *On Government.* Michael Grant, tr. New York: Penguin Classics, 1994.

Cicero, *On the Good Life.* New York: Penguin Classics, 1971.

Marcus Aurelius, *Meditations.* A.S.L. Farquharson, tr. Oxford: Oxford University Press, 1989.

Marcus Aurelius, *Meditations.* George Long, tr. New York: Avon Books, 1993. (Both this and the preceding title are good paperback editions of the *Meditations.*)

Seneca, *Moral and Political Writings.* John M. Cooper and J.F. Procope, eds. Texts in the History of Political Thought Series. Cambridge, England: Cambridge University Press, 1995.

As to the art of Pompeii, see the detailed study by Theo. Feder:

Feder, Theo. H. *The Great Treasures of Pompeii and Herculaneum.* New York: Abbeville Press, 1978.